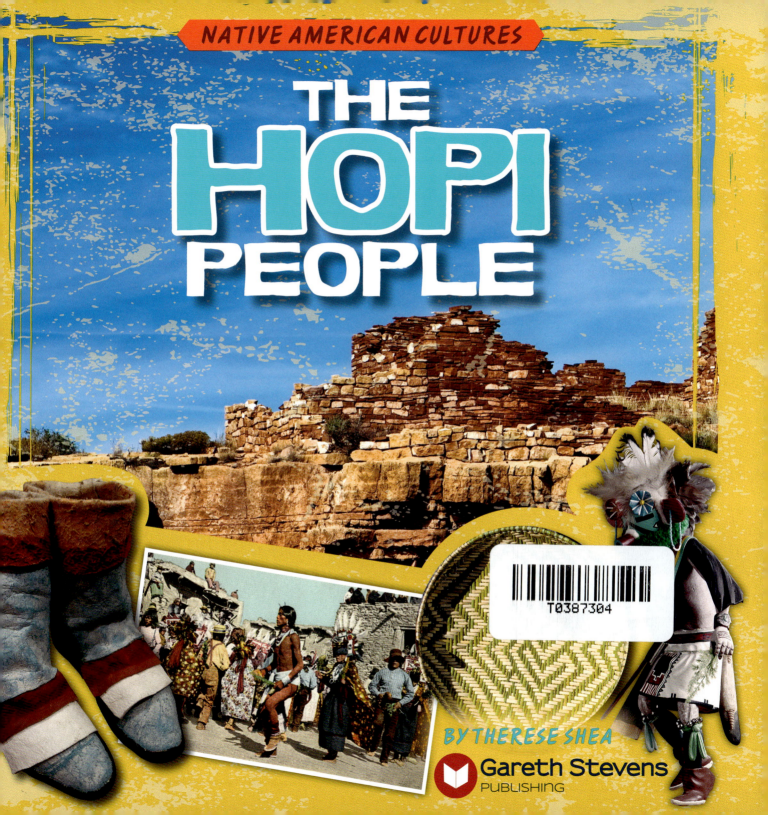

Please visit our website, www.garethstevens.com. For a free color catalog of all our high-quality books, call toll free 1-800-542-2595 or fax 1-877-542-2596.

Library of Congress Cataloging-in-Publication Data

Shea, Therese.
 The Hopi people / Therese Shea.
     pages cm. — (Native American cultures)
 Includes index.
ISBN 978-1-4824-1986-3 (pbk.)
ISBN 978-1-4824-1985-6 (6 pack)
ISBN 978-1-4824-1987-0 (library binding)
1. Hopi Indians—History—Juvenile literature. 2. Hopi Indians—Social life and customs—Juvenile literature. I. Title.

E99.H7S516 2015
979.1004'97458—dc23

2014026083

First Edition

Published in 2015 by
Gareth Stevens Publishing
111 East 14th Street, Suite 349
New York, NY 10003

Copyright © 2015 Gareth Stevens Publishing

Designer: Sarah Liddell
Editor: Therese Shea

Photo credits: Cover, p. 1 (main image) Klaus Lang/All Canada Photos/Getty Images; cover, p. 1 (moccasins) Daderot/Wikimedia Commons; cover, p. 1 (harvest dancers) Curt Teich Postcard Archives/Contributor/Getty Images; cover, p. 1 (basket) Education Images/Contributor/ Universal Images Group/Getty Images; cover, pp. 1 (Kachina), 19 Superstock/Superstock/ Getty Images; p. 4 Ævar Arnfjörð Bjarmason/Wikimedia Commons; p. 5 John Cancalosi/Photolibrary/ Getty Images; p. 7 James Gritz/Photographer's Choice RF/Getty Images; p. 9 Evans/Stringer/Hulton Archive/Getty Images; pp. 11, 15 (snake priest), 23 photo courtesy of the Library of Congress; pp. 13 (main), 15 (main) UniversalImagesGroup/Contributor/Universal Images Group/Getty Images; p. 13 (inset) Fæ/Wikimedia Commons; p. 17 Print Collector/Contributor/Hulton Archive/ Getty Images; p. 20 Robert F. Sisson/National Geographic/Getty Images; p. 21 Transcendental Graphics/Contributor/Archive Photos/Getty Images; p. 25 US National Archives bot/ Wikimedia Commons; p. 27 Rainer Lesniewski/Shutterstock.com; pp. 28–29 JaumeBG/ Wikimedia Commons.

All rights reserved. No part of this book may be reproduced in any form without permission in writing from the publisher, except by a reviewer.

Printed in the United States of America

CONTENTS

The Peaceful Hopi 4

The Ancestral Pueblo 6

Enter the Spanish 8

Many Jobs 10

Hopi Homes 12

Hopi Dress 14

Clans and Societies 16

Growing Up Hopi 18

Kachinas 20

The Snake Dance 22

Reservation 24

Self-Government 26

Visiting the Hopi 28

Glossary 30

For More Information 31

Index 32

Words in the glossary appear in **bold** type the first time they are used in the text.

THE PEACEFUL HOPI

The Hopi (HOH-pee) are a group of Native Americans who mostly live in Arizona today. They're the westernmost Pueblo Indians. These natives were named after their permanent, or lasting, settlements called pueblos.

The **ancestors** of the native peoples in North America are believed to have come from eastern Asia, perhaps as many as 12,000 years ago. They likely walked over a land bridge that existed between Asia and North America, an area now covered by the Bering Strait.

BERING STRAIT

ALASKA

SIBERIA

DID YOU KNOW?

In the Hopi language, *hopi* means "peaceful person."

Today's Hopi live much like other people in the United States. However, they still honor ancient **traditions** from time to time.

THE ANCESTRAL PUEBLO

Ancestors of native peoples moved in all directions, settling in many areas. Some settled in the desert land that's now the southwestern United States. They became farmers and built **irrigation canals** to carry water to their crops. These Ancestral Pueblo, or Anasazi, are thought to be the ancestors of the Hopi.

The Ancestral Pueblo built homes within cliffs. Some of these are still standing today. The most famous are at Mesa Verde National Park in Colorado. They were **inhabited** between AD 600 and 1300.

DID YOU KNOW?

The Hopi call their ancestors *Hisatsinom* (ee-SAH-tse-nom), which means "Ancient People."

It's thought that all Pueblo peoples are related to the Ancestral Pueblo. These are Ancestral Pueblo homes.

ENTER THE SPANISH

Around AD 1050, the Ancestral Pueblo who became the Hopi settled in what is now northwestern Arizona. That's where Spanish explorers first found them in the 1540s.

In the 1600s, Spanish **missionaries** arrived to spread the Christian **religion** to the Hopi. Spanish settlers also came to live in what they considered their new territory.

Most of the Hopi didn't want to accept the new **culture**. They and other Pueblo peoples **revolted** against the Spanish in 1680. However, the Spanish returned just a few years later.

Even though the Hopi revolted, the Europeans changed the natives' way of life by bringing illnesses, guns, and horses to North America.

MANY JOBS

Before the Spanish arrived, the Hopi were farmers. Their main crop was corn, but they also grew beans, squash, and other vegetables and fruits. The Hopi became herders after getting sheep from the Spanish.

Men farmed and herded, built houses, made shoes called moccasins, and wove blankets and clothing. Women made baskets and pottery, cooked, raised children, cared for the elderly, and carried water to their families. This last task was a hard but important one in the desert.

DID YOU KNOW?

The Hopi grew at least 24 kinds of corn! One of their common foods was a thin cornbread called *piki* (PEE-kee).

For many centuries, Hopi men grew cotton that they spun into thread and wove into cloth.

HOPI HOMES

The Hopi lived in houses made of stone and adobe, which is a mix of earth and straw baked into hard bricks. Adobe kept the house cool in the summer and warm in the winter. Homes were connected, like in an apartment building. Each family had an upstairs and downstairs with several rooms. The downstairs was mostly used for storage. The upstairs was the main living area.

Some traditional Hopi houses are still used today. Other Hopi families live in modern homes and apartment buildings.

DID YOU KNOW?

The Hopi word *ha'u* (hah-uh) means "hello."

The Hopi people used ladders to reach upstairs rooms.

HOPI DRESS

In hot weather, Hopi men usually wore a **breechcloth**, while women wore a dress called a manta that joined at the shoulder. Both wore deerskin moccasins. In colder weather, they wore blankets and leggings.

Before they were married, Hopi women wore their hair specially arranged over their ears (see picture on next page). After they were married, they wore two long braids. Hopi men usually tied a cloth band around their head. Most men wore their hair in a bun, but by the early 1900s, many cut their hair at the shoulder.

DID YOU KNOW?

The Hopi began to wear silver earrings, bracelets, and rings in the 1800s, after learning to work metal from the Spanish. Today, they're famous for their silver jewelry.

Some Hopi painted their faces and wore special headdresses for certain ceremonies.

15

CLANS AND SOCIETIES

Every Hopi belonged to a clan, a group of families. When a Hopi man married, he became part of his wife's clan and lived with his wife's family. A village might be made up of more than two dozen clans. Each village had a chief, called a *kikmongwi*. Today's *kikmongwis* are religious leaders.

The Hopi belonged to societies that had certain duties to perform, such as guarding the village and carrying out ceremonies. All men belonged to at least two societies. There were societies for women, too.

Clans and societies worked together to put on special ceremonies. Here, the Hopi perform the Flute Ceremony, which asks for rain and a good crop of corn.

GROWING UP HOPI

Traditionally, Hopi babies stayed indoors for the first 19 days of their life. On day 20, the baby was given a name during a ceremony at sunrise.

Hopi children grew up much like any other children. They played with toys. Girls received baby dolls as gifts, while boys received bows and arrows. By playing with these, they prepared for roles as mothers and hunters.

The children also did chores to help their parents. Boys learned to hunt, grow crops, and weave cloth. Girls learned to grind corn, bake bread, and make pottery.

Hopi women carried children on a "cradleboard" on their back.

KACHINAS

The Hopi religion has many traditions, and outsiders don't know all their beliefs. We do know that Kachinas, or Katsinas, are Hopi invisible gods, spirits, ancestors, and other life forces. Sometimes men and women dressed up as Kachinas to sing and dance in religious ceremonies. The Hopi asked Kachinas to bring rain for healthy crops.

The Hopi carve Kachina dolls, clothing them like dancers. They're used to teach children about the hundreds of Kachina spirits.

KACHINA DOLLS

The Hopi make Kachina dolls today that people can buy and collect.

Hopi dress as Kachinas in a ceremony in Arizona in 1908.

THE SNAKE DANCE

Some Hopi religious ceremonies aren't wholly known to the public because they're performed in a special chamber, or room, called a kiva (KEE-vuh).

One of the most well-known ceremonies is the Snake Dance, which takes place in August. Hopi gather live snakes. They take them into the kiva to wash them and pray with them. Then the performers dance with the snakes in their mouth and let them go free in the wild again. The Hopi ask the snakes to request rain from gods and spirits.

DID YOU KNOW?

Former US president Theodore Roosevelt watched the Snake Dance in 1913. He was even allowed into the kiva, which is an honor given to few.

Many of the Hopi ceremonies, including the Snake Dance, ask for rain, which is greatly needed to survive in the hot desert.

RESERVATION

In 1848, the United States won a war with Mexico and gained a lot of territory, including Hopi lands. In 1882, US president Chester A. Arthur created a **reservation** for the Hopi. It only covered one-tenth of the traditional Hopi land.

Soon, Hopi children were forced to go to a school away from their family. It was called the Keams Canyon Indian School. There, they learned English and had to dress and act as other American children. Sadly, the poor conditions at the school made many children sick. Some died.

DID YOU KNOW?

The Dawes Act of 1887 required Native Americans to divide their reservation land into lots for each family. The Hopi refused. They wanted to share the land as they always had.

Today, the village of Walpi on the Hopi Reservation still doesn't have running water or electricity. The people there live traditionally.

SELF-GOVERNMENT

As time went on, some Hopi continued to oppose changes to their culture, while others wanted to cooperate with the US government. These two sides sometimes fought. Once, a group even left their village to settle a new village.

In 1934, the Indian Reorganization Act allowed Native Americans to form their own governments. The Hopi Tribal Council was formed in 1936. The Hopi began to be left alone to continue their traditions as they wanted. Many today are raised in their religion and learn both the English and Hopi languages.

DID YOU KNOW?

The Hopi Reservation is surrounded by the Navajo Reservation. There are still arguments about land rights between the two tribes.

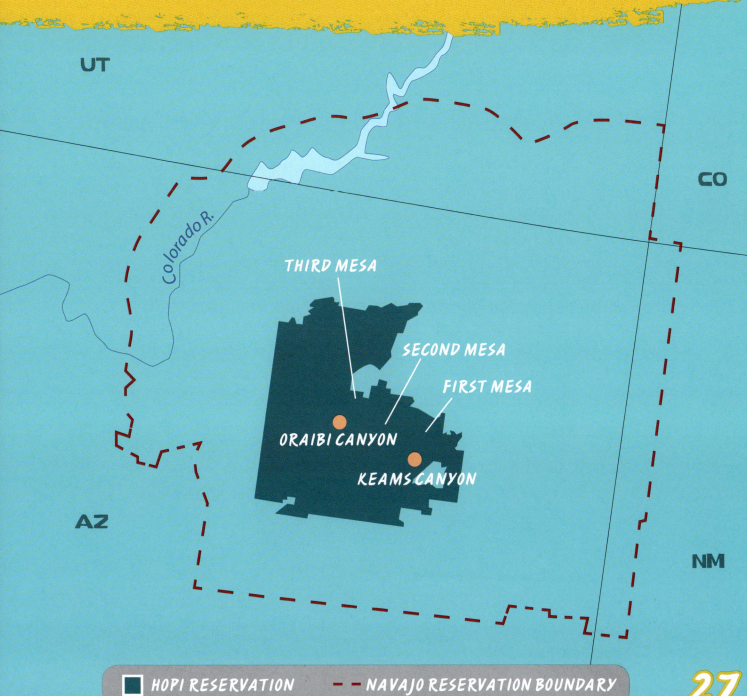

VISITING THE HOPI

Some Hopi don't allow **tourists** in their village. They think tourists upset their peaceful way of life. To learn more about the Hopi, visitors can go to the Hopi Cultural Center and Hotel on Second Mesa.

The Hopi today still have challenges to face. They must still wait for rain for their crops, just like their ancestors. There aren't enough jobs on the reservation, either. However, the Hopi continue to try to solve these problems while honoring their remarkable traditions and culture.

OLD ORAIBI

HOPI TIMELINE

1050
Ancestral Pueblo who became Hopi settle in today's Arizona

1600s
Spanish missionaries arrive in Hopi territory

1540
Spanish explorers find Hopi

1680
Pueblo revolt against the Spanish

1848
United States wins Hopi territory in war

1882
Hopi reservation established

1934
Indian Reorganization Act allows Hopi to form their own government

1936
Hopi Tribal Council Forms

2010
Population of Hopi in the United States reaches about 15,000

The oldest continuously inhabited village in the United States is located on Third Mesa. Old Oraibi, as it's called, was settled around AD 1050.

GLOSSARY

ancestor: a relative who lived long before you

breechcloth: a cloth that covers the hips

ceremony: an event to honor or celebrate something

culture: the beliefs and ways of life of a group of people

inhabit: to live in

irrigation canal: a man-made waterway used to grow plants

mesa: a flat, elevated area with steep sides that is not very large

missionary: someone sent to another country by a church to spread a religion

religion: a belief in and way of honoring a god or gods

reservation: land set aside by the US government for Native Americans

revolt: to try to overthrow an authority

tourist: a person traveling to visit a place

tradition: a long-practiced custom

FOR MORE INFORMATION

BOOKS

Bjorklund, Ruth. *The Hopi*. Tarrytown, NY: Marshall Cavendish Benchmark, 2009.

Pritzker, Barry. *The Hopi*. New York, NY: Chelsea House, 2011.

Rosinsky, Natalie M. *The Hopi*. Minneapolis, MN: Compass Point Books, 2005.

WEBSITES

Hopi Indian Fact Sheet
www.bigorrin.org/hopi_kids.htm
Read many questions and answers about the Hopi way of life.

Hopi of the Southwest
www.carnegiemnh.org/online/indians/hopi/index.html
Find out more about Hopi traditions, beliefs, and culture.

INDEX

adobe 12

Anasazi 6

ancestors 4, 6, 28

Ancestral Pueblo 6, 7, 8, 29

Arizona 4, 8, 27, 29

breechcloth 14

ceremonies 15, 16, 17, 18, 20, 21, 22, 23

children 18, 19, 20, 24

clans 16, 17

farmers 10

hair 14

herders 10

Hopi Cultural Center 28

Hopi Tribal Council 26, 29

houses 12

Indian Reorganization Act 26, 29

Kachinas 20, 21

Keams Canyon Indian School 24

kiva 22

manta 14

men 10, 11, 14, 16, 20

mesas 27

moccasins 14

Pueblo Indians 4, 7, 8, 29

religion 16, 20, 22, 26

reservation 24, 25, 26, 28, 29

revolt 8, 9, 29

Snake Dance 22, 23

societies 16, 17

Spanish 8, 10, 29

women 10, 14, 16, 19, 20